I0691151

Keeping Track of Activities

Daily Planner for Kids

Activinotes

Activinotes

DAILY JOURNALS, PLANNERS, NOTEBOOKS AND OTHER BLANK BOOKS

DATE: _____

Notes

Goal for the Day:

Important Activity for the Day:

Reminders for the Day:

Time:	Activity

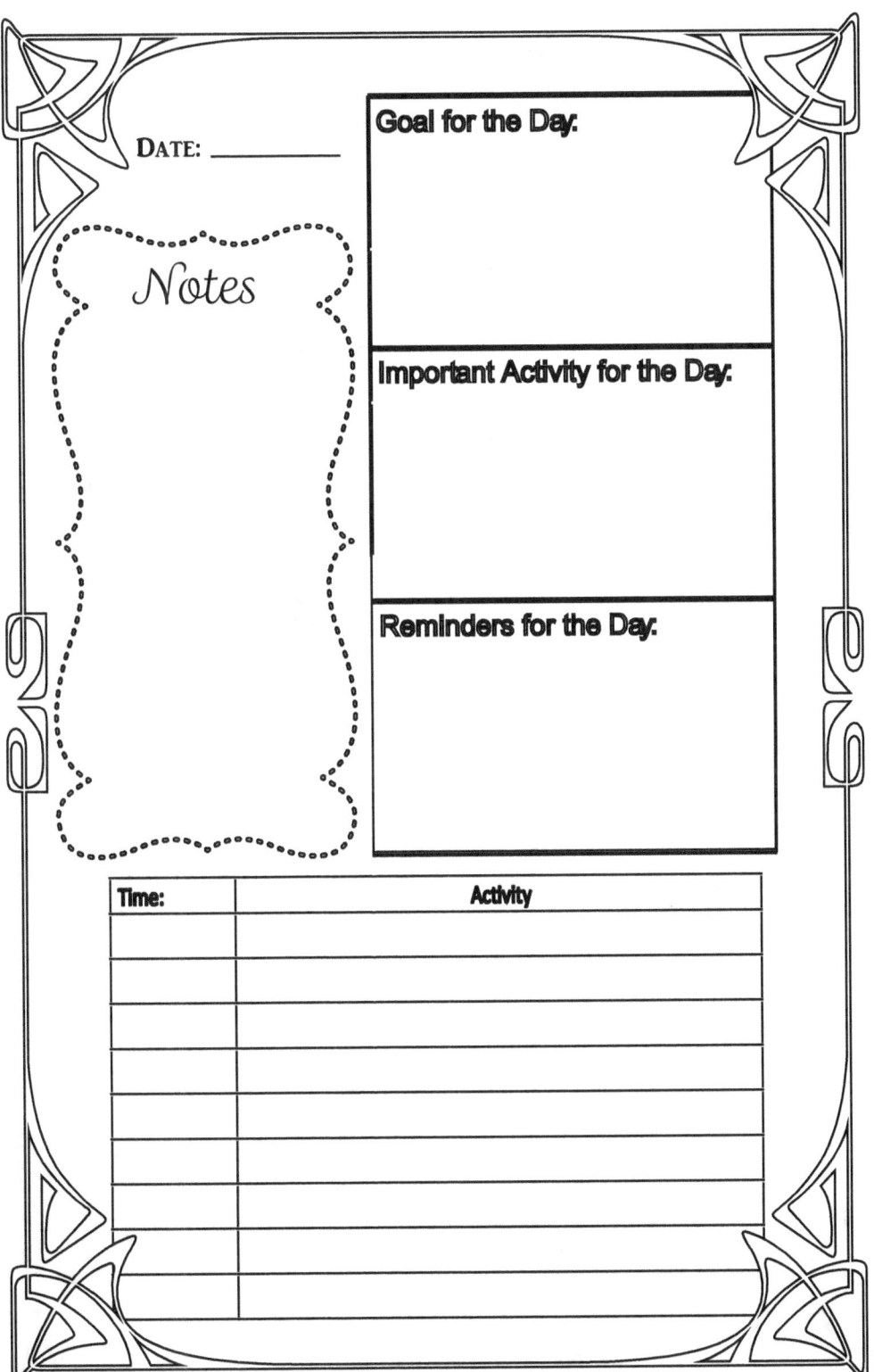

DATE: _____

Notes

Goal for the Day:

Important Activity for the Day:

Reminders for the Day:

Time:	Activity

DATE: _____

Notes

Goal for the Day:

Important Activity for the Day:

Reminders for the Day:

Time:	Activity

DATE: _____

Goal for the Day:

Important Activity for the Day:

Reminders for the Day:

Notes

Time:	Activity

DATE: _____

Goal for the Day:

Notes

Important Activity for the Day:

Reminders for the Day:

Time:	Activity

DATE: _____

Goal for the Day:

Important Activity for the Day:

Reminders for the Day:

Notes

Time:	Activity

DATE: _____

Notes

Goal for the Day:

Important Activity for the Day:

Reminders for the Day:

Time:	Activity

DATE: _____

Notes

Goal for the Day:

Important Activity for the Day:

Reminders for the Day:

Time:	Activity

DATE: _____

Goal for the Day:

Notes

Important Activity for the Day:

Reminders for the Day:

Time:	Activity

DATE: _____

Notes

Goal for the Day:

Important Activity for the Day:

Reminders for the Day:

Time:	Activity

DATE: _____

Notes

Goal for the Day:

Important Activity for the Day:

Reminders for the Day:

Time:	Activity

DATE: _____

Notes

Goal for the Day:

Important Activity for the Day:

Reminders for the Day:

Time:	Activity

DATE: _____

Goal for the Day:

Notes

Important Activity for the Day:

Reminders for the Day:

Time:	Activity

DATE: _____

Notes

Goal for the Day:

Important Activity for the Day:

Reminders for the Day:

Time:	Activity

DATE: _____

Notes

Goal for the Day:

Important Activity for the Day:

Reminders for the Day:

Time:	Activity

DATE: _____

Goal for the Day:

Notes

Important Activity for the Day:

Reminders for the Day:

Time:	Activity

DATE: _____

Notes

Goal for the Day:

Important Activity for the Day:

Reminders for the Day:

Time:	Activity

DATE: _____

Notes

Goal for the Day:

Important Activity for the Day:

Reminders for the Day:

Time:	Activity

DATE: _____

Notes

Goal for the Day:

Important Activity for the Day:

Reminders for the Day:

Time:	Activity

DATE: _____

Notes

Goal for the Day:

Important Activity for the Day:

Reminders for the Day:

Time:	Activity

DATE: _____

Notes

Goal for the Day:

Important Activity for the Day:

Reminders for the Day:

Time:	Activity

DATE: _____

Notes

Goal for the Day:

Important Activity for the Day:

Reminders for the Day:

Time:	Activity

DATE: _____

Goal for the Day:

Notes

Important Activity for the Day:

Reminders for the Day:

Time:	Activity

DATE: _____

Notes

Goal for the Day:

Important Activity for the Day:

Reminders for the Day:

Time:	Activity

DATE: _____

Notes

Goal for the Day:

Important Activity for the Day:

Reminders for the Day:

Time:	Activity

DATE: _____

Notes

Goal for the Day:

Important Activity for the Day:

Reminders for the Day:

Time:	Activity

DATE: _____

Goal for the Day:

Notes

Important Activity for the Day:

Reminders for the Day:

Time:	Activity

DATE: _____

Goal for the Day:

Important Activity for the Day:

Reminders for the Day:

Notes

Time:	Activity

DATE: _____

Goal for the Day:

Notes

Important Activity for the Day:

Reminders for the Day:

Time:	Activity

DATE: _____

Notes

Goal for the Day:

Important Activity for the Day:

Reminders for the Day:

Time:	Activity

DATE: _____

Notes

Goal for the Day:

Important Activity for the Day:

Reminders for the Day:

Time:	Activity

DATE: _____

Notes

Goal for the Day:

Important Activity for the Day:

Reminders for the Day:

Time:	Activity

DATE: _____

Notes

Goal for the Day:

Important Activity for the Day:

Reminders for the Day:

Time:	Activity

DATE: _____

Notes

Goal for the Day:

Important Activity for the Day:

Reminders for the Day:

Time:	Activity

DATE: _____

Notes

Goal for the Day:

Important Activity for the Day:

Reminders for the Day:

Time:	Activity

DATE: _____

Goal for the Day:

Notes

Important Activity for the Day:

Reminders for the Day:

Time:	Activity

DATE: _____

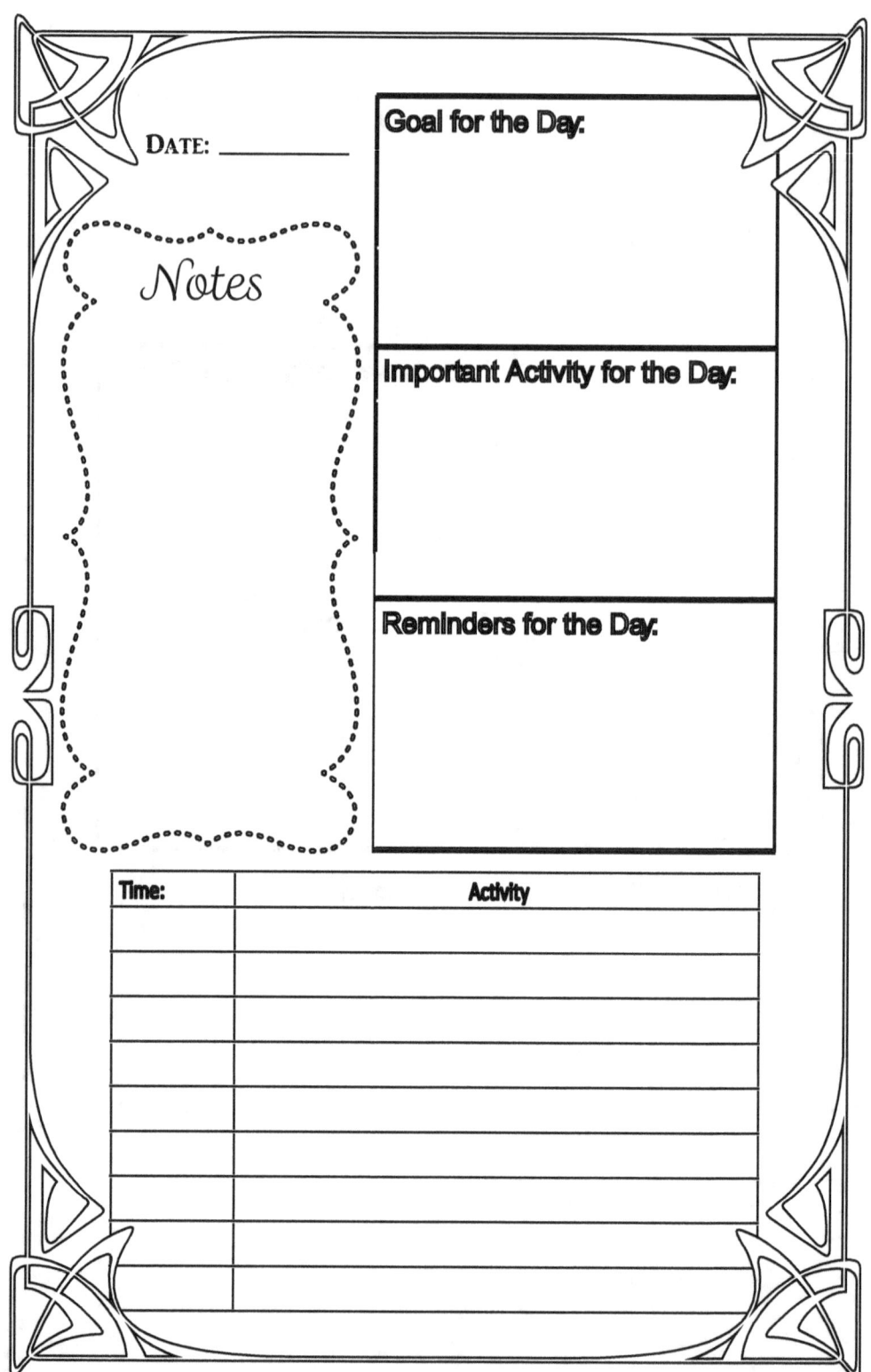

Goal for the Day:

Notes

Important Activity for the Day:

Reminders for the Day:

Time:	Activity

DATE: _____

Goal for the Day:

Notes

Important Activity for the Day:

Reminders for the Day:

Time:	Activity

DATE: _____

Notes

Goal for the Day:

Important Activity for the Day:

Reminders for the Day:

Time:	Activity

DATE: _____

Notes

Goal for the Day:

Important Activity for the Day:

Reminders for the Day:

Time:	Activity

DATE: _____

Notes

Goal for the Day:

Important Activity for the Day:

Reminders for the Day:

Time:	Activity

DATE: _____

Notes

Goal for the Day:

Important Activity for the Day:

Reminders for the Day:

Time:	Activity

DATE: _____

Notes

Goal for the Day:

Important Activity for the Day:

Reminders for the Day:

Time:	Activity

DATE: _____

Goal for the Day:

Notes

Important Activity for the Day:

Reminders for the Day:

Time:	Activity

DATE: _____

Notes

Goal for the Day:

Important Activity for the Day:

Reminders for the Day:

Time:	Activity

DATE: _____

Notes

Goal for the Day:

Important Activity for the Day:

Reminders for the Day:

Time:	Activity

DATE: _____

Notes

Goal for the Day:

Important Activity for the Day:

Reminders for the Day:

Time:	Activity

DATE: _____

Notes

Goal for the Day:

Important Activity for the Day:

Reminders for the Day:

Time:	Activity

DATE: _____

Notes

Goal for the Day:

Important Activity for the Day:

Reminders for the Day:

Time:	Activity

DATE: _____

Notes

Goal for the Day:

Important Activity for the Day:

Reminders for the Day:

Time:	Activity

DATE: _____

Notes

Goal for the Day:

Important Activity for the Day:

Reminders for the Day:

Time:	Activity

DATE: _____

Notes

Goal for the Day:

Important Activity for the Day:

Reminders for the Day:

Time:	Activity

DATE: _____

Notes

Goal for the Day:

Important Activity for the Day:

Reminders for the Day:

Time:	Activity

DATE: _____

Notes

Goal for the Day:

Important Activity for the Day:

Reminders for the Day:

Time:	Activity

DATE: _____

Notes

Goal for the Day:

Important Activity for the Day:

Reminders for the Day:

Time:	Activity

DATE: _____

Notes

Goal for the Day:

Important Activity for the Day:

Reminders for the Day:

Time:	Activity

DATE: _____

Notes

Goal for the Day:

Important Activity for the Day:

Reminders for the Day:

Time:	Activity

DATE: _____

Notes

Goal for the Day:

Important Activity for the Day:

Reminders for the Day:

Time:	Activity

DATE: _____

Notes

Goal for the Day:

Important Activity for the Day:

Reminders for the Day:

Time:	Activity

DATE: _____

Notes

Goal for the Day:

Important Activity for the Day:

Reminders for the Day:

Time:	Activity

DATE: _____

Goal for the Day:

Notes

Important Activity for the Day:

Reminders for the Day:

Time:	Activity

DATE: _____

Notes

Goal for the Day:

Important Activity for the Day:

Reminders for the Day:

Time:	Activity

DATE: _____

Goal for the Day:

Important Activity for the Day:

Reminders for the Day:

Notes

Time:	Activity

DATE: _____

Notes

Goal for the Day:

Important Activity for the Day:

Reminders for the Day:

Time:	Activity

DATE: _____

Notes

Goal for the Day:

Important Activity for the Day:

Reminders for the Day:

Time:	Activity

DATE: _____

Notes

Goal for the Day:

Important Activity for the Day:

Reminders for the Day:

Time:	Activity

DATE: _____

Goal for the Day:

Notes

Important Activity for the Day:

Reminders for the Day:

Time:	Activity

DATE: _____

Notes

Goal for the Day:

Important Activity for the Day:

Reminders for the Day:

Time:	Activity

DATE: _____

Notes

Goal for the Day:

Important Activity for the Day:

Reminders for the Day:

Time:	Activity

DATE: _____

Notes

Goal for the Day:

Important Activity for the Day:

Reminders for the Day:

Time:	Activity

DATE: _____

Notes

Goal for the Day:

Important Activity for the Day:

Reminders for the Day:

Time:	Activity

DATE: _____

Goal for the Day:

Important Activity for the Day:

Reminders for the Day:

Notes

Time:	Activity

DATE: _____

Notes

Goal for the Day:

Important Activity for the Day:

Reminders for the Day:

Time:	Activity

DATE: _____

Notes

Goal for the Day:

Important Activity for the Day:

Reminders for the Day:

Time:	Activity

DATE: _____

Notes

Goal for the Day:

Important Activity for the Day:

Reminders for the Day:

Time:	Activity

DATE: _____

Goal for the Day:

Notes

Important Activity for the Day:

Reminders for the Day:

Time:	Activity

DATE: _____

Goal for the Day:

Notes

Important Activity for the Day:

Reminders for the Day:

Time:	Activity

DATE: _____

Goal for the Day:

Important Activity for the Day:

Reminders for the Day:

Notes

Time:	Activity

DATE: _____

Notes

Goal for the Day:

Important Activity for the Day:

Reminders for the Day:

Time:	Activity

DATE: _____

Notes

Goal for the Day:

Important Activity for the Day:

Reminders for the Day:

Time:	Activity

DATE: _____

Goal for the Day:

Notes

Important Activity for the Day:

Reminders for the Day:

Time:	Activity

DATE: _____

Notes

Goal for the Day:

Important Activity for the Day:

Reminders for the Day:

Time:	Activity

DATE: _____

Notes

Goal for the Day:

Important Activity for the Day:

Reminders for the Day:

Time:	Activity

DATE: _____

Goal for the Day:

Notes

Important Activity for the Day:

Reminders for the Day:

Time:	Activity

DATE: _____

Goal for the Day:

Important Activity for the Day:

Reminders for the Day:

Notes

Time:	Activity

DATE: _____

Notes

Goal for the Day:

Important Activity for the Day:

Reminders for the Day:

Time:	Activity

DATE: _____

Notes

Goal for the Day:

Important Activity for the Day:

Reminders for the Day:

Time:	Activity

DATE: _____

Notes

Goal for the Day:

Important Activity for the Day:

Reminders for the Day:

Time:	Activity

DATE: _____

Notes

Goal for the Day:

Important Activity for the Day:

Reminders for the Day:

Time:	Activity

DATE: _____

Notes

Goal for the Day:

Important Activity for the Day:

Reminders for the Day:

Time:	Activity

DATE: _____

Notes

Goal for the Day:

Important Activity for the Day:

Reminders for the Day:

Time:	Activity

DATE: _____

Notes

Goal for the Day:

Important Activity for the Day:

Reminders for the Day:

Time:	Activity

DATE: _____

Goal for the Day:

Important Activity for the Day:

Reminders for the Day:

Notes

Time:	Activity

DATE: _____

Notes

Goal for the Day:

Important Activity for the Day:

Reminders for the Day:

Time:	Activity

DATE: _____

Goal for the Day:

Important Activity for the Day:

Reminders for the Day:

Notes

Time:	Activity

DATE: _____

Notes

Goal for the Day:

Important Activity for the Day:

Reminders for the Day:

Time:	Activity

DATE: _____

Goal for the Day:

Important Activity for the Day:

Reminders for the Day:

Notes

Time:	Activity

DATE: _____

Goal for the Day:

Notes

Important Activity for the Day:

Reminders for the Day:

Time:	Activity

DATE: _____

Notes

Goal for the Day:

Important Activity for the Day:

Reminders for the Day:

Time:	Activity

DATE: _____

Notes

Goal for the Day:

Important Activity for the Day:

Reminders for the Day:

Time:	Activity

DATE: _____

Notes

Goal for the Day:

Important Activity for the Day:

Reminders for the Day:

Time:	Activity

DATE: _____

Goal for the Day:

Important Activity for the Day:

Reminders for the Day:

Notes

Time:	Activity

DATE: _____

Notes

Goal for the Day:

Important Activity for the Day:

Reminders for the Day:

Time:	Activity

DATE: _____

Notes

Goal for the Day:

Important Activity for the Day:

Reminders for the Day:

Time:	Activity

www.ingramcontent.com/pod-product-compliance
Lightning Source LLC
Chambersburg PA
CBHW080737250626
47170CB00010B/2857